IT IS WELL

Claudia Myrie

DEDICATION

My dearest Louise (warrior). Years ago, I questioned what I could give to my daughter, that in the future would remind her that she was loved. So I wrote her a book. When writing this book, God reminded me of this and told me to dedicate this book to you! May you remember that you are not forgotten, you are loved, and that it is well!

Abba, thank you for trusting me with your download! It's an honor to do your will.

To Jonny and Kerry, I appreciate you both and cannot express enough my gratitude for your prayers and friendship.

To The Watch family, this season of consecration has literally been my lifeline! Apostle Tobi and Pastor Nicola, if you ever get discouraged please remember that your sacrifice has not gone unnoticed. Thank you.

Elisha, you have literally gone through all the seasons of my life with me! And lord knows there's been many! You have taught me the truth in the scripture proverbs 18:24, there truly are some friends that stick closer than a brother. Thank you for sticking!

Maryse, it could only be you that I could dream of a friendship with, without even knowing you! I could never have imagined it being so deep, so quickly! Your passion to see people free inspires me daily! Thank you

INTRODUCTION

Firstly, I want to start by saying how much the term 'it is well' has previously irritated me and how insensitive I found it! God truly had to work on my heart, and heal aspects of it for me to have a different perspective. Before I begin, ask that the spirit of God moves over you and that your heart is softened enough to hear what Abba has for you in this book!

May today be the day you start your healing and faith journey! It is well!

This short book is based around 2 kings 4:8-37, about the Shunamite woman! I hear you asking, how can you write a whole book based around a woman without a name? Simple answer, because on the 5th of February 2023, God said so! He placed it in my heart how important this message was, so it felt unfair to not share it. Sharing is caring and all that.

IT IS WELL

Going forward in this book, you'll notice that I take each of these scriptures step by step and break it down because I find it all relevant, and I'm hoping after the breakdown you'll also understand why; I'd be interested to know what the Holy Spirit says to you about each verse. I'd like to disclose that this isn't going to be your usual type of 'Christian book' with extremely profound discoveries that you'd need a Rabbi, Priest, and a Monk to decipher. It's rather basic principles to help you walk this journey called life, with the understanding that you are God's child. Even if right now, you can't feel that.

One thing I'm learning is that we are all simply vessels. I say this because everything I say in this book has come from an imperfect vessel. I give examples and share my own personal experiences, so I plead with you to read the word of God for yourself and allow God to speak to you through your vessel.

CHAPTER ONE

MAKE ROOM FOR GOD

2 Kings 4:8-37 comes directly after the story about the widow's oil. I encourage you to read this because that's a very good read! In fact, I may do my breakdown on that passage too. However, our chosen scripture focuses on a woman of or from Shunem, The Shunammite woman.

The scripture starts with Elisha, who was a prophet, just going through Shunem and meeting this woman. I love the fact that in verse eight in other versions

IT IS WELL

(NIV, AMP, and NKJ) it says the woman was influential, well-to-do, and respected! This is about someone who had what she wanted. She wasn't in a place of 'earthly need' but always made room, and time, and hosted Elisha.

This made me realize the importance of creating space for God and being an instrument of service. We live in a world where everything is so fast-paced, and we constantly strive for more, whether it would be a success, a new car, a new job, or a new house, the list is endless, sometimes making room for God is put on a back burner! We give God our last fruits instead of our first, we are overwhelmed, overworked, overstimulated, we've got a backlog of things to do, which never seems to go down, and let's not forget to mention the reels we scroll through that allows us to only process 20 seconds of information! It's a challenge, right? I'm here with you, but let's look at the scripture, with all of this woman's influence, she was intentional about making room for God and his people. This may be a season that requires you to take time to assess your life and what you've made a priority! Does it truly have to be there? Are you operating a little like Martha when God wants you to be more like Mary and sit at his feet (Luke 10:38-42). Imagine cooking and cleaning for the creator of the world, when you can just sit at his feet and worship!

In our fast-changing world, everything has been designed to capture our attention and if we are not careful enough, God might be one of those things that will suffer in our lives. Have you ever gone for a day or two without opening your Bible or taking some moments to talk to God? It's possible, so I'm not judging.

Sometimes, we might even be caught up with religious activities without making a proper place in our hearts for God. He deserves and desires our best.

IT IS WELL

He wants to be the first in your life. God is a jealous God and he wouldn't allow anyone or anything to take his place as the lord over our lives.

In Luke 10:38-42, Jesus visits the home of two sisters, Martha and Mary, and he teaches them the importance of making a place for God in their lives. While Martha is busy with household chores, Mary sits at Jesus' feet, listening to his teachings. Jesus says to Martha, "Martha, Martha, you are worried and upset about many things, but only one thing is needed. Mary has chosen what is better, and it will not be taken away from her." It's interesting that Martha was rather annoyed with Mary, asking Jesus to get her to help, and questioned whether he was aware of her needs. Isn't that much like us today, being resentful of others who've chosen the 'soft life' because we're busy, exhausted, and completely run down!

IT IS WELL

Just like the Shunamite woman and Mary, we too can make a place for God in our lives by putting aside our worries and distractions and focusing on him. When we make a place for God in our lives, we open ourselves up to his love, wisdom, and blessings.

Making a place for God in our lives requires sacrifice and commitment, but it is worth it. When we prioritize our relationship with God, everything else falls into place. Our worries and distractions will always be there but our perspective on them will change, and we will experience peace, joy, and purpose in our lives.

So, let us follow the examples of the Shunamite woman and Mary, and make a place for God in our lives. Let us open our hearts to his love, and allow him to fill our lives with his peace, joy, and purpose.

IT IS WELL

"But seek first his kingdom and his righteousness, and all these things will be given to you as well." - Matthew 6:33

When we make a place for God in our life, God is committed to making a place for us, not only in the world but in the world to come. Jesus told his disciples, "in my father's house there are many mansions"

CHAPTER TWO

BE SPIRITUALLY MINDED

The scripture makes us understand that God is spirit, and anyone that should worship him must do so in the spirit. Spiritual things are discerned spiritually. We can see from 2 kings 4:9-10 that the woman is clearly spirit-filled as a revelation has been shown to her that Elisha was a Holy man. She acts out her conviction and requests to create space for him every time he comes. In this day and age and as someone in charge of safeguarding at my church, this sounds absolutely wild to me! But I don't want us to miss the importance of this verse. It takes discernment to recognize someone else who is spirit-filled.

We can at times focus on the negative people around us and have adopted a culture of canceling people, I mean, we all know people that every new year update with their chest all the people that are toxic around them, and that year they'll be blocking folks! Hmmm...no shade, but that could be you! It's ok, there's grace! What I'm saying is that we can slip into the rabbit hole of focusing on the negative that the positive is right in front of you and you may not recognize it because your judgment dial is switched to recognizing the negative. I don't want to pass this topic so lightly because this may be due to some traumas in your life that need intervention. Please seek help and ask the Holy Spirit to reveal this to you, so you can begin to heal from this.

IT IS WELL

In addition, it takes empowerment from the spirit of God for us to do the will of the Father. The early church was told to wait until the outpouring of the spirit upon them before they began to spread the gospel to nations around them. Even though they had the zeal for God's work, they needed to wait for the release of the spirit before they engage in the work of the ministry.

Much of the chaos that happens in life and ministry today is because we try to use the natural mind to comprehend spiritual things and the Bible says, a natural man cannot comprehend things of the spirit because they are foolishness unto him.

Moving down the verses 11-13 of the same second kings chapter four. It's so interesting that there are so many lessons to be learned from this story, however, the woman is nameless and only referred to as the Shunammite woman. Now, I hear all the 'feminist spirits' popping up, which I exit the stage left on because, the fact that this woman makes it in the bible and is highly revered by Jewish rabbis tells me, there wasn't an issue of mentioning her name because she was a woman! However, her name didn't seem to be a major factor. There are many different perspectives as to why her name wasn't mentioned, I, personally haven't had a revelation on it and as this is an interactive book, I'd love to hear your thoughts on this! There are however links to say that the son she later conceives is Habakkuk, who is a minor prophet. However, her work and heart preceded her name. So I ask, do you want what you do to be recognized and your name added to it, or do you want your heart to carry on through generations?

CHAPTER THREE

RESPECT SPIRITUAL AUTHORITY

My next point in this verse is one that may make you want to put this book down and allow your pride to get the better of you! Yes, I said it! There is an importance in respecting men and women of God, we are all equal I hear you say! To that comment, I respectfully roll my eyes! Listen, this is coming from someone that has struggled in this area for years! Check those thoughts, and go deeper! Don't stop until you allow yourself to be truthful with yourself!

IT IS WELL

Yes, I'm aware of scriptures such as Galatians 3:28 There is neither Jew nor Greek, there is neither slave nor free, there is no male and female, for you are all one in Christ Jesus.

Galatians 1:27 "So God created man in his own image, in the image of God he created him; male and female he created them."

Acts 10:34 "So Peter opened his mouth and said: "Truly I understand that God shows no partiality,"

Romans 10:12 "For there is no distinction between Jew and Greek; for the same Lord is Lord of all, bestowing his riches on all who call on him."

Oh, I can keep going on, but what I'm talking about is not whether God loves us the same or not. Of course, He does! It's more about having different responsibilities in the kingdom of God. 1 Corinthians 12:27 talks about us being a body and having different parts. If we have different roles, we then can't function equally, so I reinforce my statement and ask that we give honor where it's due.

It was because of honor and respect that we later see in this scripture how the woman was blessed. So I ask you to check your heart. If you are really struggling to respect men and women of God and can't seem to figure out why, I plead that you find someone that you trust, that is spirit filled, be honest with them, and ask them to pray for you. You may discover that there is a root, which needs to be dealt with.

We have been given a commandment to honor, not just our spiritual leaders and mentors, but all men and women of God. Yes, all! See, if you have to honor someone because of what you can get or because the person is high up there, then is the honor genuine? We are to honor all men and women of God, even those that don't look like it. The honor you have for God shows in how you treat people around you, especially people that may not necessarily be able to do anything for you.

God is never a biased God, however, for the sake of order, He gave the ministry gifts to some. Then some were chosen by grace for greater responsibility and as such deserve to be honored for laying down their lives for the cause of the gospel. One of the reasons why we need to honor our spiritual leaders is because they represent God and his intent.

Disrespect can cost you your life. You may be familiar with the story of Elisha, who a group of young boys began to mock and tease, calling him bald. Elisha was not angry at the children, but he prayed that God would teach them a lesson, they doubted God and disrespected the man of God. God answered Elisha's prayer and two bears came out of the forest and attacked the 42 youths.

CHAPTER FOUR

BE COMMITTED TO SERVING GOD

Another thing we saw the Shunammite woman demonstrate is that she had a heart of hospitality. The woman positions herself with a giving heart to not be forgotten and this is a sign of spiritual maturity because God is love, and every lover gives. I can appreciate that hospitality is not easy for everyone! God blessed me with a gift and grace of hospitality, especially when it comes to my home but there are definitely times I don't always feel like doing it.

IT IS WELL

Now, I'm not saying we should always allow people into our homes and spaces, definitely not! That's just unwise! But I'm talking about those times when I've slapped my layers of clothes on, put up my hoodie, etched a 'do not approach me' look on my face, and marched through my area, being very aware that I've purposely positioned myself in a space of 'don't talk to me, I'm not here for it'! I see you, my passive-aggressive siblings, God's still working on us. Hospitality comes in so many ways that the best way this woman could show this was to create a physical space for Elisha. Take time today to work out how you can show hospitality towards things that build the kingdom.

Elisha was clearly overwhelmed by her generosity as he felt she deserved to be rewarded for this. There are many people that walk through life feeling disregarded and unappreciated, I want to encourage you to not get weary of doing good as the bible says

IT IS WELL

(Galatians 6:9) Let us not become weary in doing good, for at the proper time we will reap a harvest if we do not give up. God sees you and in His time he will be your rewarder!

She offered her generosity because she simply wanted to! She didn't want any other possessions, she was already well-to-do and respected. From this I ask, do we give freely? Are we carrying a tally chart of what we want back as we give? I stand by my comment that God will reward your good works but to make every giving about what you're about to receive appears disingenuous.

2 Kings 4:14-15 The woman had a need but it may have not happened for so long that she pushed it aside and continued serving God despite her need. I think we can all safely say that there are things that we have prayed for that we haven't received, now that may be because the prayer wasn't in line with

the will of God, which is why it is so important to know the will of God which can only be learned through his word, no escaping folks! The word of God is foundational to our faith.

I used to have a youth leader who would say from Archeology to Zoology, the bible has it all, the answers are there, and we can no longer continue to plead ignorance when we have access to so much knowledge in one book! Heck, those in the western world where we have access to the internet at a simple click of a button, what's really our excuse for not knowing or at least seeking? Cue the section that it gets heavy; we can sometimes place our identity in our weaknesses, I say this because I've noticed, starting with myself, I can at times go on a "woe is me" rant, feeling sorry for myself and not wanting to come out of my vicious cycle of a victim mentality because the truth is, it's easier!

IT IS WELL

There are no expectations of me, when I'm in the pit, I don't have to strive and I can continue to make excuses for where I am and why I should stay here! Now, I know this may sound insensitive but believe me, I've had my fair share of trials slapped on me from the day I was born, and I'm not writing to say I am where I know God wants me to be, no! But I refuse to stay down! I refuse to watch those I love, play victim for the rest of their lives, living unfulfilled menial existences because they've been knocked down.

I have absolutely no idea how I got here, but I sense that God wants us to wake up, heal and move forward. So many people are tied to our destiny and the life we choose is slowing down the work of God and p.s. you are NOT showing humility playing this kind of small! It's actually a form of pride, now, I know I'm snatching a few edges here, but I mean you well! You take this righteous anger you feel towards me right now and let it push you to change! Get up! Arise!!!

CHAPTER FIVE

UNDERSTAND HOW PRAYER WORKS

Prayer is the master key as we know it to be, but there are principles to engage for our prayers to be effective. God answers all prayers but we must be discerning to know what he's saying because his answers to prayers are not always "yes". The scripture explains that all promises of God are yes and amen, this tells us that God is only committed to getting his will done on earth.

IT IS WELL

We can also learn from the Shunammite woman because she wasn't the one that said what she wanted. Sometimes a prayer can go unanswered for so long we may even begin to forget about it! But God! He's heard it all. Through this part, I ask you to resurrect any old dreams, visions, and goals you've prayed for that haven't been answered and take them back before the cross! Before you do this though, I ask you to assess your request, is it in line with the will of God, trust me, some people are praying for some questionable things! Whatever you're praying for, have you gone through God's principles to attain this? For example, you want a business, have you researched about the business you want, have you taken the steps to invest in your business idea, have you set it up? Or are you in your room praying that God gives this to you?

Now, you can see what I'm driving at. There are so many biblical principles that can be applied when building wealth or a business and if we don't know what that is; like I said, go back to the word and pray for wisdom so you receive your revelation! If this was my desire I would rather pray for wisdom and open doors and I apply those biblical principles, there's a requirement from you. Don't sit down and expect it to be handed to you by some divine miracle but you haven't remotely even considered the principles! Be honest with yourself. Would you give such a responsibility to yourself?!!

The Shunammite woman's need of having a child, other than the obvious, but she couldn't do anything else but pray and trust God! She could remind God of his promises but that would be it. The rest requires God's hand. The woman at this stage still hadn't been the one to say she wanted this to the prophet, this is to remind you that God hears you. Even when you no longer have any words. He hears you.

IT IS WELL

2 Kings 4:16 now, this section, would be for those of us that have a prophetic gift, to be honest, I believe that's all of us but that's another book. I love the specificity of Elisha's prophecy! He was clear with the details of what he was saying.

Now, I don't know about you but I've been to some services and the word preached or prophesied to me has confused me more than the UK government (joking, not joking), men and women of God, if you have received a word for someone, I urge you to please pray and ask for a revelation before you share! Now, there are times when a word would only make sense to the person you are giving it to! But I'm tired of hearing about flying pigs and unicorns on a pink cloud and then forcing my head down to receive your word! That's confusion and we need to show reverence to God and his giftings. I believe these ratchet moves are what makes unbelievers mock us and God's gift. We need to do better!

IT IS WELL

Back to the scripture, I can actually imagine the genuine shock it would have been for the Shunammite woman to have heard that a prayer she'd prayed for and could only be answered as a miracle as her husband was old, was going to happen! The Bible is clear with what she said, but in modern-day translation, I could hear her saying, my friend, don't play with me!!

In verse 17, true to Elisha's word, she conceives a boy and this here should give us hope! God is still in the business of answering prayers. From firsthand, from someone who had so many fertility issues, I am a testament to God answering prayers! I've had many miscarriages, false hopes, and heck even lost my left Fallopian tube but I have a beautiful daughter, who can only be destined for great things! In fact, I'm making a bold step like Elisha to say that I'll conceive again! I say all of this to express the importance of God's appointed time is crucial!

CHAPTER SIX

HAVE FAITH IN GOD

Now here's where the story gets heavy and changes! We all like a good cliffhanger, so hold unto your seats! From 2 kings 4:19-25, I read this section over and over again as although something traumatic has happened, where her son dies, it's obvious that she's not carrying the weight that would be expected. I struggled to let go of how deep this is and I hope it penetrates for you too! I can't even lose my keys for 2.5 seconds without having a panic attack! How does this woman lose her son? Her God's gift and carry on like nothing has happened. The only answer I can think of is faith! The trust that God gave it to her, so this couldn't be the end! Whoa, that's heavy!

Now, for me personally, there's a lot for me to contend with because like I've just mentioned, I was not supposed to lose my children, because it was God's gift, I've also experienced a mother lose her child at birth and witnessed that unquenchable grief, was that child not God's blessing?! The truth is, I don't have the answers to that and I don't suspect anyone can give you answers that will soothe the pain and trauma of these experiences and whatever you may be going through; I just need to let you know that God mourns with us! I also know that this pain was never his plan for us, and living in a fallen world that brings us so many unanswered questions, we have a God that we can go to and get that deep healing and comfort he wants to give us.

IT IS WELL

Going back to this woman, I ask what sort of faith would it be that everyone around her is in shock and mourning and she's not allowing this to phase her and simply says 'it is well'! Not it will be well but 'it is well'! With those words, she spoke into her past, present, and future! This was the moment that this sentence changed its meaning for me! Physically things may not seem ok, but because of our faith and trust in our father, we can boldly say 'it is well'! Please don't negate the healing you have to do, it's actually crucial to your future that you heal and not bleed over anyone you encounter or worse operate through the pain because that could be detrimental to the kingdom, but we are called to have confidence in our 'It is well'

Moving back to our selected scripture verse 25-26 I love that this woman was proactive! She was not going to sit down and allow this situation to penetrate without taking action. Faith without works is dead, we need to come out of the mindset of believing that we don't have a part to play in our lives, too many of us waiting for a miracle or chasing prophecies but never acting on anything and then having resentment declaring to anyone that would listen that God has not heard you!

The woman has obviously continued her generosity towards the prophet as he recognized her and he still held her in high regard, especially to the point of getting someone to run to her. This woman teaches us about being genuinely consistent with our work. Sometimes God blesses us with our hearts desires and then the thing he blesses you with becomes the reason you step away from God or are not as committed, come on we all know that sister that prayed for her husband, and as soon as she got married, no one sees her at a prayer meeting or that brother that prayed and fasted for a job and now, he's chooses to work on weekends and no one sees him anymore, or my personal favorite parents who pray for children and then says, 'I've got to focus on what God has blessed me with, these children take a lot of our time', so can not come to church or any church events, this is no judgment, I've fallen into all of those traps, I'm just your annoying friend that wants to help us all to do better! A loyal heart comes despite your situation.

The woman when being asked what was wrong as to why she was there, replies again with 'it is well' she clarifies and reinforces her faith, I love that she repeats this here! Basically what she's saying is 'did I stutter?' I said it is well, so it is well! In Verse 27 The woman shows her desperation by grabbing Elisha at his feet, this eradicates any theories, that the woman is in a state of shock that she doesn't realize what's happening! She's perfectly aware, this was the moment she expresses her distress.

IT IS WELL

This is another one for us believers, to learn to be more sensitive to others needs. Elisha at this moment needed discernment to reveal her distress. It is so important as believers to not always go by what a person is acting out but by what's happening in their hearts.

I know it's hard when someone is giving you stress and grief, it's hard to not get in our feelings, I mean, I've been known to say, that my sister/brother really wants me to go south London on them, but that's not the way! We need the Holy Spirit so we don't treat people so unkindly and reciprocate their energy because of their actions.

In verse 28 this woman means business, she is bold as she holds the man of God accountable for what he spoke. She takes him back to his word. This confirms the importance of knowing God's words! We can stand on those scriptures when in need, but because of the lack of knowledge, we perish.

In verse 29 this section is where the scripture obedience is better than sacrifice rings true! Elisha tells Gehazi to go to the house where this child is and put his staff on the child's face but before he did that, whilst en route, he should literally not talk or greet anyone even if they spoke to him! In this, I'm spoken to about not allowing yourself to be contaminated by things of the world, even if it doesn't appear to be politically or socially acceptable. There comes a point in our life we receive strict and clear instructions from God and it may seem weird to others but crucial we heed those instructions. Sometimes it's necessary to cut yourself off from people to be obedient to God, ouch! Painful right? Now, I'm not talking about difficult characters that God may have put in your life to refine you, so don't use this as a pass to be using your blocking card! In all things be led!

In verse 30 we learn something about this woman's nature! She did not get to where she was by being a pushover, no sir!! She had fire in her stomach, she says and for this, I've got to quote it; "As the Lord lives, and as your soul lives, I will not leave you." So he arose and followed her."

II Kings 4:30 she was not allowing Elisha just to walk away from his word and not honor it! This reminds me of when Jacob says to the Angel of God, I won't let go until you bless my soul! Now this cost him, he was left with a broken hip but similar to this, this woman was radical! She has a righteous anger that causes the hand of God to move. This is why I don't believe we're supposed to be playing passive roles in our destinies! We can not keep laying flat while we have back-to-back issues and not fight!! We are warriors, we are called to put on our full armor of God and fight back!

Elisha didn't have a choice, he ended up following her because she made it very clear she wouldn't be going anywhere! How persistent are we when it comes to the things of God? Where is our tenacity?

So in verse 31 when Gehazi followed instructions and comes back, he still didn't come back with good news. Gehazi was unable to see a change in the boy's situation! This was a wake-up call for me, we need to recognize that It's not everyone that has or is the answer to your prayers, sometimes our faith ends in the hands of someone that was never supposed to be our answer.

I love in every version of the scripture that it says the child had not awakened or revived! I believe the woman's reaction caused others not to speak death over her son. They had to get in line with what she said! 'It is well'. This is an encouragement to you all to rebuke any words spoken over you, we live in a society where labeling has become the foundation of everything, it's like we have to label any identity that we don't understand, more so that things can make sense, but I ask, make sense for who? Everyone has an agenda so taking on their labels without questioning the source is frightening! The Bible speaks about the power of the tongue, do not allow labels to be pronounced over you, your children, or your friends and family. A label could have defined the end!

When Elisha goes to see the child in verses 32-33 he soon sees the gravity of the situation. He, at this moment, knew the prayers he would need to pray. This would need to be a miracle. The fact that the child was lying on his bed, became his responsibility.

IT IS WELL

This is a real lesson to us people of God to be very mindful of the words and prayers we give out! It's not every day talking with no accountability! We must be held accountable for everything we say, not to say we can't make mistakes, of course not but accountability is necessary.

"And he went up and lay on the child, and put his mouth on his mouth, his eyes on his eyes, and his hands on his hands; and he stretched himself out on the child, and the flesh of the child became warm. He returned and walked back and forth in the house, and again went up and stretched himself out on him; then the child sneezed seven times, and the child opened his eyes."

2 Kings 4:34-35 The process of this is so intriguing! Although the boy became warm, it wasn't completed yet! Many stop when they get a hint of a breakthrough. At times there is so much more! We

hear the acronym PUSH (pray until something happens), but I challenge us to keep praying even after this.

After the boy was warm, Elisha still paced up and down the house, keeping in the spirit, then again went to stretch himself out on him, until....only then was he given a sign! The boy sneezes 7 times and the number 7 signifies completion! Until Elisha received his sign, he couldn't go anywhere. The question I ask is have you become so excited about the warmth that you didn't wait for the fire? Have we moved on too prematurely?

CONCLUSION

Now we're at the end of this story where the boy comes back to life and the Shunammite woman is called back into the room to take her child! But we can underestimate the power of what just happened! That God who raised this child is still the same God! He still raises people from the dead and works other miracles that no one but him can do! May we never forget to honor our father.

Now, I know throughout this book I've given you some difficult pills to swallow and it's not because I'm an expert in these areas, believe me, I'm working through all of these points daily, so I encourage you to not lose sight of the main points revealed to us,

1) Always make room for God, let's stop putting our creator at the end of our things-to-do list and commit to giving him our first fruits.

2) May we pray for discernment so we are regularly spirit-led. Let's get out of this culture of canceling people, let's leave that to the world

3) Respect men and women of God, learn the importance of submission, and give honor where it's due.

4) Remember the importance of giving and hospitality, emphasizing the scripture Hebrews 13:2 (NIV) Do not forget to show hospitality to strangers, for by doing so some people have shown hospitality to angels without knowing it. What a powerful

scripture to know that by giving back out what God gives to us, we will be doing our part in the kingdom.

5) Pray even when facing adversity and include God's will as you pray. Refuse not to close your eyes to the principles of God and be led in your prayers.

6) We use our mustard size faith to confess 'it is well' despite what the situation looks like. Just like Job, we refuse to curse God in the worst of our situations, or like Jacob, you can say 'I won't let go until you bless my soul' even if it means there are physical consequences!

With all the carrots and sticks in this book, I hope you can begin to see the light at the end of the tunnel in your situation, my prayer is that you place God above your situation and ask to borrow his eyes so you can see what he feels about that situation and how much he loves you

IT IS WELL

Once you've received your blessing, never forget God's love language of gratitude! The Shunammite woman recognizes the miracle before her and worships accordingly. May we never forget the miracles and answered prayers we've been given and praise and worship for those blessings!

NOTES

NOTES

NOTES

NOTES

NOTES

NOTES

NOTES

NOTES

Printed in Great Britain
by Amazon

18282920R00034